ANNE FRANK IN THE WORLD 1929-1945

COMPILED BY THE **ANNE FRANK** HOUSE

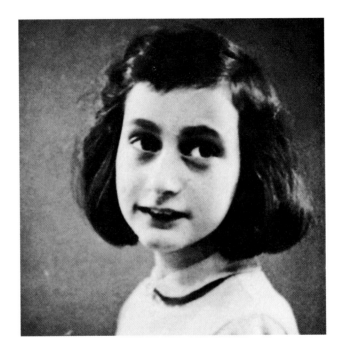

ALFRED A. KNOPF

NEW YORK

ANNE FRANK IN THE WORLD

1929

1945

COMPILED BY THE **ANNE FRANK** HOUSE

THIS IS A BORZOI BOOK PUBLISHED BY ALFRED A. KNOPF

Original text copyright © 1985, 1989, 1992, 1994 by the Anne Frank House
Revised text copyright © 2001 by the Anne Frank House
Foreword copyright © 2001 by Rabbi Julia Neuberger
Photographs copyright © see acknowledgment on page 142
All rights reserved under International and Pan-American Copyright Conventions.
Published in the United States of America by Alfred A. Knopf, a division of
Random House, Inc., New York. Distributed by Random House, Inc., New York.
Originally published by the Anne Frank House, Amsterdam, the Netherlands, 1985 under the title *De Wereld van Anne Frank
1929–1945* to accompany the international traveling exhibition of the same name. This edition is based on the original text translated
from the Dutch.
Published in Great Britain by Macmillan Publishers Limited, 2001.
KNOPF, BORZOI BOOKS, and the colophon are registered trademarks of Random House, Inc.

www.randomhouse.com/kids

Library of Congress Cataloging-in-Publication Data
Anne Frank in the World
p. cm.
ISBN 0-375-81177-X (trade) — ISBN 0-375-91177-4 (lib. bdg.)
1. Jews—Germany—History—1933–1945—Juvenile literature. 2. National socialism—Juvenile literature. 3. Jews—Persecutions—
Netherlands—Juvenile literature. 4. Holocaust, Jewish (1939–1945)—Netherlands—Juvenile literature. 5. Frank, Anne, 1929–1945—
Juvenile literature. 6. Germany—Ethnic relations—Juvenile literature. 7. Netherlands—Ethnic relations—Juvenile literature. [1. Jews—
Persecutions—Germany. 2. Jews—Persecutions—Netherlands. 3. Holocaust, Jewish (1939–1945). 4. National socialism. 5. Frank,
Anne, 1929–1945.]
DS135.G3315 A55 2001
940.53'18—dc21
2001029148

Printed in the United States of America
October 2001
10 9 8 7 6 5 4 3 2 1
First American Edition

FOREWORD

by Rabbi Julia Neuberger

A few years ago, I was talking to a school group about being Jewish and what that meant to me. After I had explained that my mother was a refugee from Nazi Germany, a child asked me whether I thought Anne Frank was the most famous Holocaust survivor. I was stunned by the question. After all, Anne Frank perished in Bergen-Belsen in 1945, age fifteen. But the more I thought about it, the more I realized that the boy was right. Anne Frank *is* the most famous Holocaust survivor. But what survived was her diary, an intimate journal that led to her memory becoming in some way eternal, as people came to understand what the war against the Jews meant through the words of one young teenager.

In this collection of photographs of Anne Frank's world, we get a sense of what things were like during her lifetime. There is the bustling city of Frankfurt, home to one of Germany's largest Jewish communities, including much of my own family. The Frank family went to the Netherlands to escape the worst of the Nazi measures. Many of my own family went to the Netherlands, to England (and survived), to Palestine (and became among the earliest Israelis), and wherever else they could go. But many of them were murdered or died of disease, starvation, and cruelty in the concentration camps or on the unimaginably ghastly journey to them, without water, toilet facilities, proper ventilation, or adequate space. My elderly great-grandmother was deported in her bedridden state. Cousins of my father, elderly teachers who were badly off, perished because they could not get out. And there were many more.

Visiting Frankfurt's Jewish Museum today, with its long list of Frankfurt Jews who perished, I can see what happened to one side of my family. The other side is less well remembered. There are boxes of photographs of people I never knew, which my mother has painstakingly labeled with their names so that they will not be forgotten when she dies. And there are a few members of the enormous Rosenthal family still scattered around the world.

There are thousands upon thousands of Jews who can tell a similar story. The refugees and survivors are themselves now very elderly, telling their stories urgently because they do not want to die with their own experience unrecorded. But soon they will be gone. Which is why Anne Frank's diary, and the tale it tells of surprising domesticity amid horror and destruction, is so important. She would have been in her seventies now had she lived, but we see her always as a young girl, full of optimism, full of fears as well, with a wicked sense of humor, ever youthful.

Her story is well known. She wrote her diary from her thirteenth birthday until forced to stop when the hiding place in which her family and friends had been safe for some two years was raided by the SS on August 4, 1944. The eight people hiding in the Annex at 263 Prinsengracht, Amsterdam, were taken prisoner, along with two of their helpers. The eight in hiding were Anne; her older sister, Margot; her parents, Otto and Edith; Hermann and Auguste van Pels and their son, Peter (whom Anne, thinking she might someday turn her diary into a novel, called the van Daan family), from Osnabrück in Germany; and the latecomer, Fritz Pfeffer, a dentist (Albert Dussel in the diary), also originally from Germany. Anne observed them closely, and her strictures on Dussel make for hilarious reading. He had the reputation of adoring children but in fact did little but criticize all three young people—and hog the one and only lavatory for large parts of the day. In a less-than-kind moment—and one can see why her fellow residents in the Annex did not always think Anne was kind—Anne wrote a timetable for Mr. Dussel's use of the lavatory:

Dussel now sits on the "bog," to borrow the expression, every day at twelve thirty on the dot. This afternoon, I boldly took a piece of pink paper and wrote:

Mr. Dussel's Toilet Timetable:
Mornings from 7:15 to 7:30 A.M.
Afternoons after 1:00 P.M.
Otherwise, only as needed!

I tacked this to the green lavatory door while he was still inside. I might well have added "Transgressors will be subject to confinement!" because our lavatory door can be locked from both the inside and the outside.

Not the most charitable of entries in Anne Frank's diary, but utterly human. This was someone who had the thoughts we all have, the resentments we all have, the burgeoning sexuality and complaints about her parents all teenagers have. Her very normality, so beautifully expressed, is what makes her diary so memorable. And this volume of photographs showing her world and how it fell apart gives one a sense of the normal becoming extraordinary, the safe becoming threatening, the opening up of the world becoming a confinement. We see here the rise of Nazism in Germany, the use of hatred to unify the Germans, the rapid suppression of the trade union movement, the killing of those with mental disability, the easily won support of the churches.

Hitler's rise to power demonstrates how a clever and ruthless leader can turn a country's institutions into racist endeavors in a very few short years. Of course, it would not have happened if there were not a low level of anti-Semitism under the surface. It would not have happened if more people had been brave, or even cared. But the fact is, it turned out to be remarkably easy.

And although the churches objected to the killing of the mentally unfit, most did not object to the killing of the Jews, including those who had converted to Christianity.

So what can we learn? Unfortunately, all too much. This collection of photographs makes it clear that it was also not difficult for the Nazis to enforce anti-Semitic laws in the Netherlands after the invasion. Yet the Netherlands had been a hospitable home for the Jews since the end of the fifteenth century. Resistance took time to build up—though the resistance movement in the Netherlands did, in fact, help to hide many Jews later on. But there was no immediate leadership, such as there was in Denmark from the royal family, which made it impossible for the Nazis to destroy the Jews there. When news came that Denmark's small Jewish population was to be rounded up and deported, the extraordinary Danish resistance movement, with the help of other citizens, transported almost all of the country's Jews to neutral Sweden. Very few nations behaved as well as Denmark, though many individuals in all parts of Europe risked their lives and their welfare to help.

The Netherlands became increasingly anti-Semitic. No one had expected the invasion so early, and the Dutch had anticipated being neutral, as they had been in the First World War. Nobody had expected that the Germans would behave as well as they did when they first occupied the Netherlands. Later German occupation was a reign of persecution, terror, and starvation, but the early days were quiet, almost peaceful, and the Dutch, surprised by this, were relatively compliant at the outset.

This volume chronicles all this in great detail. We see Nazism on the rise in Germany and then again in the Netherlands. We see German Jews who had distinguished-service medals from fighting for their country in the First World War wearing those same medals outside their shops as boycotts led to *Jude* (Jew) being painted on the windows. My grandfather had fought for Germany and been a prisoner of war in the First World War. What was he to make of his old friends, his fellow prisoners of war, cutting him dead in the street during his last two years in Germany before emigration?

The Franks were being pursued by people who espoused that foul ideology of racial hatred—and eventually they were betrayed, despite the wonderful people who helped them, two of whom were themselves imprisoned. Indeed, one of the lessons of Anne Frank's life and death, and of this volume of photographs of her world, is that there were always good people, though often they were few and far between. The four helpers who hid the Frank family were good people. The British consul in Frankfurt, Frank Foley, who signed so many visas for desperate Jews, was a good person. The Swedish diplomat in Hungary, Raoul Wallenberg, whose ultimate fate is unknown but who rescued thousands of Jews, was a good person. The Portuguese consul, Aristides de Sousa Mendes, who signed visa after visa for safe passage to Portugal despite instructions telling him not to, was a good person. And there were many, many more.

It is this innate goodness in humanity, despite the terrible things that human beings can do to each other, that the Anne Frank House—the permanent memorial and museum into which the hiding place at 263 Prinsengracht has been turned—celebrates so successfully. There you can see what humanity can do at its worst, but you can also celebrate what it can do at its best, and what individuals can do in the face of great adversity if they are governed by a strong moral code and have courage and empathy with those who are suffering.

But despite all that good, all that optimism about human nature on which Anne Frank's diary relies, of the eight people who were hidden, all but Otto Frank perished. He then dedicated the rest of his life to publishing his daughter Anne's diary, which had been rescued from the floor of the Annex by Miep Gies, one of their protectors, and to setting up the Anne Frank House with its universal anti-racist message. Anne Frank's story is about anti-Jewish action and sentiment certainly, but it is also about the danger of creating outsiders, of shaming them, of making them wear particular signs or carry particular identity cards.

In our own day, there are others who are viewed as outsiders—and many of us collude with that. They may be asylum seekers and refugees, challenging the West's immigration restrictions in a powerful way as they flee from terror and oppression or from economic disaster or just from a lack of hope. They may be people with severe mental illness or with learning disabilities. They may be the Gypsies—the Roma—of Europe. They may be all sorts of people toward whom the bulk of society decides to show no hand of friendship, no tolerance.

The real message of Anne Frank's diary is about tolerance, and the lesson we find so difficult today is that tolerance can mean giving something up, doing more than speaking pleasant platitudes—it is about allowing in, sharing, being true friends to those we do not know. Governments need to show leadership when popular sentiment is intolerant and to demonstrate that racist talk has no place in any of our societies, that hatred leads to terrifying violence and destruction, as Anne Frank's story demonstrates. The lesson of her story is that refugees should be made welcome and the persecuted given a helping hand.

Most people, if given half a chance, will revert to an almost animal love of their own tribe and hatred and fear of others. You have only to look at the former Yugoslavia, at the Hutu and Tutsi in Rwanda, at the new racists in Germany, and at anti-asylum-seeker demonstrations in Ireland. It is a universal problem. Otto Frank hoped his daughter's diary would somehow lead to hope, lead to change, lead to people saying, "Never again." He was too optimistic, too convinced the message would get through of just how terrible the Nazi war against Jews, Gypsies, homosexuals, and others really was.

The lesson of these photographs, the lesson of Anne Frank's story, is that there are always hatreds, always those who wish to pick on particular groups and make them scapegoats for the world's ills. The lesson of Anne Frank is that each of us must do all we can to counter that, whatever our ethnicity, religion, or country of origin. As Anne Frank made abundantly clear, though she did not live to see it, the future is in our hands—and we are able to make it a tolerant one or a racist one, by our actions or lack of them.

CONTENTS

THE FRANK FAMILY

Members of the Frank family have lived in Frankfurt since the 17th century. Otto Frank is born on May 12, 1889, in the city's Westend, a well-to-do neighborhood. After attending high school, he briefly studies art at the University of Heidelberg. Then, via a friend, in 1908 he is offered and accepts a job in the United States, at Macy's department store in New York City. After the death of his father, a banker, Otto returns to Germany in 1909 and works for a metal engineering company in Düsseldorf until 1914. During World War I, Otto and his two brothers serve in the German army, where Otto attains the rank of lieutenant. After the war, he works in his father's bank, but banks are not doing well at that time. It is during this period, however, that Otto meets his future wife, Edith Holländer, the daughter of a manufacturer. Edith was born in 1900 and grew up in Aachen. In 1925, Otto and Edith marry and settle in Frankfurt. Their first daughter, Margot Betti, is born on February 16, 1926. Her younger sister, Anne, whose full name is Anneliese Marie, is born in Frankfurt on June 12, 1929.

2

3

4

1 *A family portrait, circa 1900. Otto Frank, wearing a sailor suit, is sitting in the front row, third from the left.*
2 *Otto Frank (right) and his brother Herbert in the German army, 1916.*
3 *Edith Holländer.*
4 *Edith and Otto during their honeymoon in San Remo, on the Italian Riviera, 1925.*

Otto Frank is an enthusiastic amateur photographer. He takes dozens of photographs of Anne and Margot playing in the street with their friends, visiting their grandparents in Aachen, or going to the countryside.

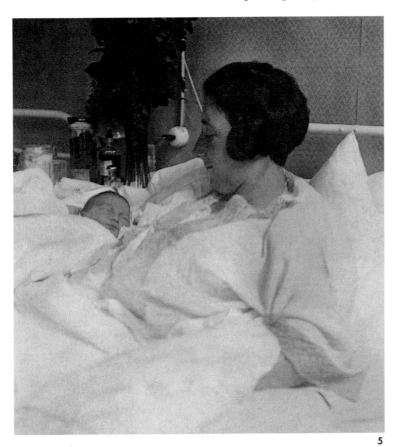

5

5 Anne Frank at one day old with her mother, Edith, June 13, 1929.
6 Margot admires her new sister, July 1929.
7 Margot and Anne.
8 Anne with her mother at the Franks' apartment on Ganghoferstrasse, Frankfurt am Main, 1931.

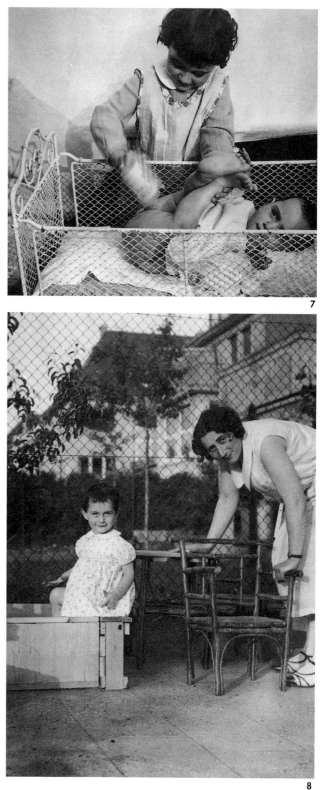

7

8

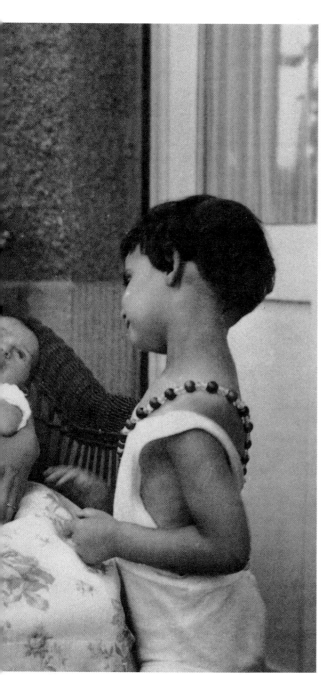

6

9 *Anne sleeping.*
10 *Anne and Margot with their father, Otto, 1931.*
11 *Anne and Margot.*
12 *Edith, Anne, and Margot near the Hauptwache (the old guardhouse) in Frankfurt's city center, 1933.*
13 *Anne, 1932.*

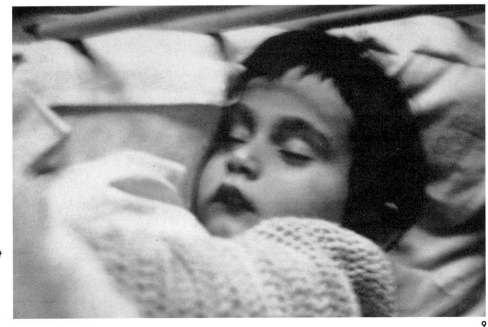

9

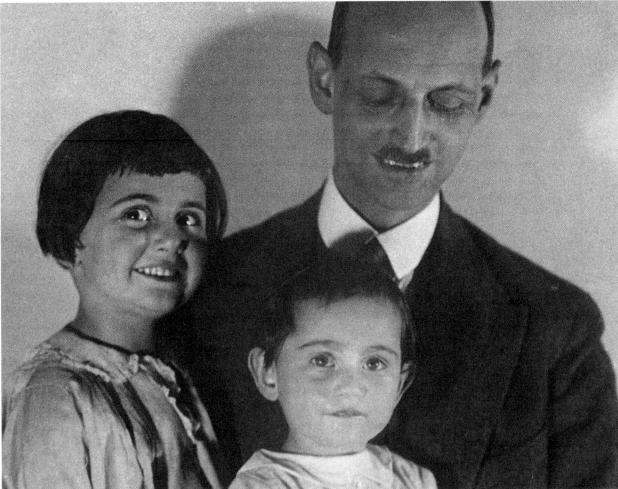

10

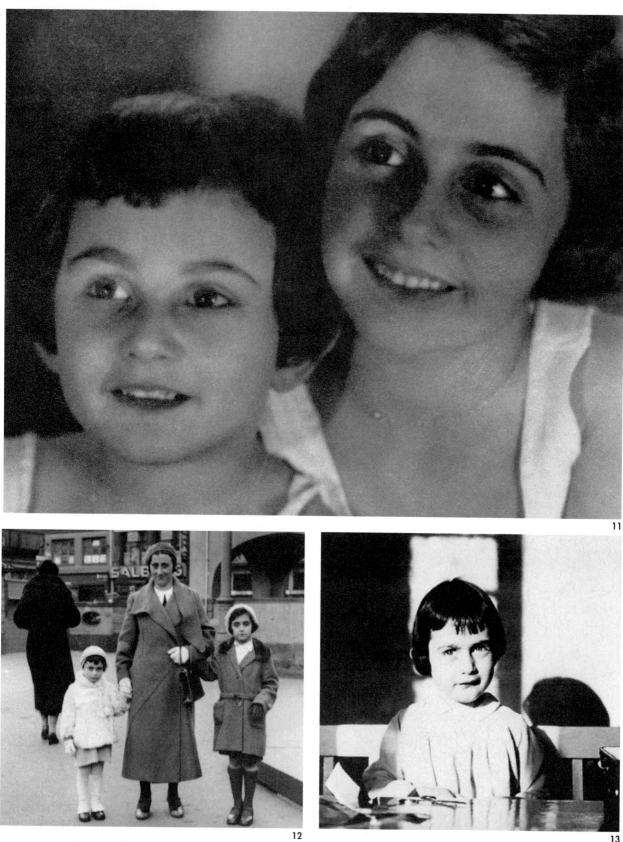

11

12

13

FRANKFURT AM MAIN IN THE 1920s:
A PORTRAIT OF THE CITY

Frankfurt is situated on the river Main and has been an important center of trade and finance since the Middle Ages. New industrial areas sprang up on the east and west sides of the city at the end of the 19th century, and by the end of World War I, Frankfurt has absorbed its surrounding villages to become Germany's largest city in terms of land area.

In 1929, the city is home to 540,000 people. Tradition and modernization have gone hand in hand, and as a result, Frankfurt is an attractive, modern city—economically, socially, and culturally. The intellectual and political climate is democratic and liberal.

15

14 *A view of Frankfurt from the river Main, circa 1932. The spire on the left belongs to the cathedral, where German kings and emperors were crowned from 1562 until 1806.*
15 *A street in a run-down inner-city area, 1924.*
16 *New housing areas offer various facilities, including modern schools and playgrounds. Photo circa 1930.*

16

14

GERMANY IN THE 1920s: POLITICAL AND ECONOMIC CRISIS

Germany suffers from economic crises and inflation during the 1920s, following the humiliations of the country's defeat in World War I and the subsequent Treaty of Versailles. The Great Depression, which begins in 1929, causes further social and political tension. The country's democratic government—the national assembly of the so-called Weimar Republic—is unable to resolve the situation, and the German labor movement carries on the lion's share of the political struggle against extreme-right groups such as Adolf Hitler's Nazi Party (the National Socialist German Worker's Party, founded April 1, 1920).

In Frankfurt between 1929 and 1932, industrial activity drops by 65 percent. By the end of 1932, more than 70,000 of the city's population are unemployed, while a quarter no longer have a steady income. The working class is particularly hard hit.

17

17 In Frankfurt, the Nazis gather strength during the 1920s. Members of Der Stahlhelm—the anti-democratic, right-wing organization of ex-servicemen, with which the Nazis are associated—march through Frankfurt, 1925.
18 A soup kitchen for the unemployed in Frankfurt's Friedrich Ebert quarter, 1932.

19 An anti-Nazi demonstration in Frankfurt arranged by the Eiserne Front (Iron Front), an association of several left-wing organizations.

18

19

In 1929, about 30,000 Jews are living in Frankfurt—roughly 5.5 percent of the city's population. It is Germany's second-largest Jewish community after Berlin, and it dates back to the Middle Ages. Beginning in the 14th century, Jews were required to live in a walled ghetto. But at the beginning of the 19th century, this forced segregation ended and Jews were given equal rights under the law, setting in motion a process of social and cultural assimilation. Jewish philanthropic organizations played an important role in the city's development. By the early 20th century, although anti-Semitism has not completely disappeared, Frankfurt is for the most part a tolerant city. Jewish citizens are able either to maintain their traditional way of life or to assimilate into society, as they choose.

20

20 *In 1882, a synagogue was built on Börneplatz next to a huge open-air market. Photo 1927.*

21 *The Judengasse (Jewish ghetto) in Frankfurt, circa 1872. During the days of the ghetto, the street was closed every evening, and Jews were forbidden to leave.*

22 *A notice in the Kölnerhof Hotel, near the Frankfurt railway station, makes it clear that Jews are unwanted guests. Photo 1905.*

21

22

Germany's economic crisis continues into the early 1930s. Workers lose their jobs; farmers, their land; civilians, their savings. The Nazi Party profits from the situation by recruiting more and more followers. Hitler blames Germany's problems not only on the government, which he describes as weak, but also on the Jews.

Fascist movements want absolute power, through "democratic" means if possible—in other words, by obtaining as many votes as they can. Hitler shrewdly exploits the apparent need for a scapegoat for society's ills— he blames the Jews.

23 *Unemployed Germans, Berlin, 1932.*
24 *Adolf Hitler (right, seated) as a soldier at the front during World War I.*
25 *Nazi election campaign propaganda.*

24

26 The NSBO—the organization of Nazi worker groups—joins strikes in order to gain popular support.
27 The SA, or Brownshirts, grows out of the "sports division" of the Nazi Party and is formed to maintain order at Nazi meetings. Later it becomes an elite group of thugs. Joining the SA is an attractive alternative for many of the unemployed.
28, 29 In Bad Harzburg on October 11, 1931, Germany's right-wing political parties close ranks and name themselves the Harzburger Front. The combined groups demand the chancellor's resignation and new elections.

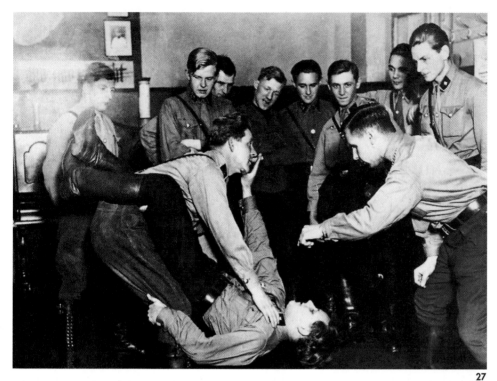

27

28

29

In 1932, Hitler wins the German elections, obtaining 37 percent of the 13.7 million votes. He heads a coalition government at first, partly because the opposition is divided, and is made chancellor of Germany in January 1933. On March 5 of that year, there is another vote, and the Nazi Party obtains 44 percent. On March 24, Hitler officially obtains absolute power with the so-called Enabling Law, which allows him to bypass the constitution and, effectively, to pass whatever law he likes. On July 14, all other parties are declared illegal.

Hitler's power is now absolute. He is effectively a dictator, supported and advised by a close circle including Joseph Goebbels and Hermann Göring as ministers of state, Heinrich Himmler as head of the SS (which under Himmler's command develops from a "protection squad" into an elite unit in charge of concentration camps, and Hitler's instrument of force) and later the police, and Reinhard Heydrich in charge of the Gestapo (the Nazis' political police force). Hitler's Germany is declared to be the Third Reich (Third Empire), the first two being those presided over by Charlemagne in the early Middle Ages and by Bismarck in the 19th century.

Hitler begins with wide popular support. The German nation's feelings of uncertainty and discontent are channeled into a mass political movement. Elsewhere in Europe, fascist and right-wing nationalist movements are also developing.

30

31

30, 31 *Nazi posters.*
32 *A Nazi, Albert Krebs, replaces the Jewish mayor of Frankfurt.*
33 *The Nazis celebrate Hitler's appointment as chancellor, Berlin, January 30, 1933.*
34 *The swastika flag is raised at the Römer, Frankfurt's town hall, March 1933.*

32

33

34

A key Nazi doctrine is the "leader principle," or *Führerprinzip,* the open rejection of parliamentary democracy. Elections are held during the early years of the Nazi regime, but for appearance sake only. All other political parties are forbidden, and political opponents are removed—in 1933, about 150,000 are sent to concentration camps for "reeducation."

36

35 Hitler addresses the Reichstag (the national assembly), October 6, 1939.
36 Even dead democrats are enemies—the statue of Friedrich Ebert, Germany's first president, is demolished, April 1933.
37 Oranienburg concentration camp near Berlin, April 6, 1933. Concentration camps are initially established to detain opponents of the Nazi party.

37

35

The Nazis soon try to disband the German labor movement, and the arrest of 10,000 active members in March 1933 is a heavy blow to the trade unions. That same month, however, in spite of terror and repression, anti-Nazi trade union groups get 80 percent of the vote in company elections.

Hitler announces the celebration of a Day of National Labor on May 1, 1933, and the confederation of trade unions advises its members to take part. The day turns into a huge pro-Nazi demonstration, however, and on May 2 the Nazis occupy the trade union buildings and seize union property throughout Germany. Trade union leaders are replaced by Nazis.

As of May 10, 1933, the German Workers' Front is the only union allowed to operate, and all workers are forced to become members. There is no longer any place in Germany for an independent labor movement that protects its members' interests. Workers and their employers must cooperate with the Nazis. Strikes are forbidden.

39

38 Communists and Social Democrats are arrested by the SA, spring 1933.
39 Throughout Germany millions of people celebrate the Day of National Labor on May 1, 1933. Photo taken in Munich.
40 On May 2, 1933, the SA takes over trade union buildings throughout the country. Photo taken in Berlin.

To fight Germany's widespread unemployment, the Reich Labor Service initiates labor projects such as the construction of freeways and the growth of the arms industry. The country's economy is put on a war footing, and everyone must contribute. Teenagers and young adults are forced to work an allotted period of time for a nominal wage, and while they are working, they are indoctrinated in Nazi ideology. From 1938 on, workers in certain professions, such as manufacturing industries and engineering, are forced to work for the war effort.

41 *On behalf of 40,000 male and 2,000 female workers, the leader of the Reich Labor Service, Konstantin Hierl (left), pledges allegiance to Hitler, September 1938.*
42 *Handing out shovels to build the freeways. Photo taken near Frankfurt, September 1933.*
43 *Men marching to work.*

42

43

Nazism is dependent upon propaganda. Mass meetings, photographs, posters, stamps—all are used to disseminate Nazi ideology. Spreading the message is considered so important that in March 1933, the Nazis even set up a Ministry for Enlightenment and Propaganda under Goebbels' leadership. This has responsibility for disseminating propaganda, curtailing the cultural activities of non-Aryans, controlling radio and the press (German and foreign), as well as film, theater, foreign writing about Germany, literature, painting and other visual arts, music, and tourism. It is probably the most important instrument of *Gleichschaltung*—the philosophy of making everyone think the same way.

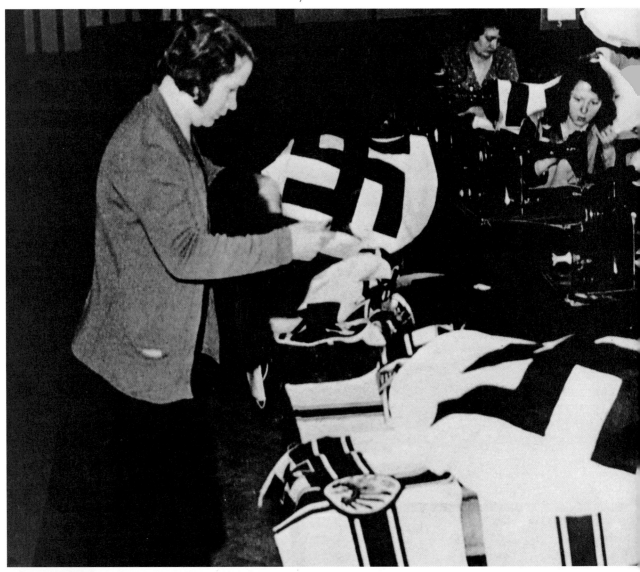

44 *A swastika flag for every household.*
45 *The Day of the Party, a gigantic annual propaganda rally, 1937.*
46 *Anti-Jewish propaganda from the extreme racist magazine Der Stürmer: "The Jews are our ruin" and "The racial question is the key to world history."*

45

44

46

On April 1, 1933, Joseph Goebbels, minister in charge of propaganda, declares an official boycott of Jewish shopkeepers, doctors, and lawyers. Ten days later, all civil servants with one or more Jewish grandparents are fired. Scores of other measures are designed to remove Jews from their jobs and businesses. According to the Nazi philosophy, there is only room for Aryans (pure-blooded white Germans) in the nation. Only Aryans can be "compatriots," or *Volksgenossen*. Jewish companies are "Aryanized"—the owners are forced to sell their property at a price fixed by the Nazis, after which the Nazis fire all remaining Jewish personnel.

47

49

48

50

51

47, 49, 50 Nazis campaign for their boycott of Jewish-owned shops and businesses. On their placards are the slogans "Germans! Defend yourselves! Don't buy from Jews!"

48 "Jew" is daubed across shop windows, Berlin, 1933.

51 A Jewish shopkeeper wearing military decorations earned fighting for Germany in World War I, in front of his store in Cologne.

In April 1933, Adolf Hitler receives a delegation of German judges. Although the judges dedicate themselves to the new order, they ask that in return for their loyalty, Hitler guarantee their independence. Hitler agrees, provided certain "necessary measures" are taken. The delegation approves his measures, and as a result, Jews and political opponents within the legal profession are fired.

A few judges realize the ramifications and retire. Others believe they can prevent a worse situation by staying on. Soon, however, the judicial system becomes part of the machinery of terror. To begin with, the judges accept the race laws and evidence obtained by torture. Then they accept the unrestricted actions of the SA, SS, and Gestapo against so-called traitors. And finally, they even accept the stripping of legal rights from Jews, homosexuals, and Gypsies.

52 A street check in Berlin, 1933. The police can stop, search, and arrest anyone they choose.
53 A member of the SA (right) serves as a police officer. This photo's original caption read "Law and order restored in the streets of Berlin."
54 The SA in action.
55 Under its president, Roland Freisler (center), the Volksgerichtshof (People's Court) condemns hundreds of people to capital punishment, sometimes for very minor offenses.

53

54

55

Although their ideology is basically anti-Christian, from 1933 onward the Nazis can count on ample support from the German churches. With few exceptions, the Protestant and Catholic churches endorse the Nazis' racial and political principles. On March 28, 1933, the Catholic bishops lift their ban on membership in the Nazi movement. The following month, Hitler is endorsed by the Altpreussische Union—the largest of the Protestant provincial church groups. With the exception of the Bekennende (Confessing) Church, the official churches fail to protest against the persecution of the Jews—even of the Jews who have converted to Christianity.

57

56 Ludwig Müller, a member of the anti-Semitic "German Christian" movement, is made Reichsbischof (imperial bishop) of the German Evangelical Church in September 1933. Here Bishop Müller is shown speaking in Berlin, September 25, 1934.

57 Church leaders salute Hitler at the Festival for the Catholic Youth of Berlin, August 20, 1933.

58 Hildegard Schaeder is a member of the Bekennende Church, along with Dietrich Bonhoeffer and Martin Niemöller. The Bekennende Church protests from the beginning against the persecution of the Jews. Bonhoeffer is arrested for helping Jews and hanged by the Nazis in April 1945. Niemöller is imprisoned in Dachau in 1938 but released in 1945. Schaeder (pictured here after the war) helps Jews to escape from Germany. Between 1943 and 1945, she is detained in Ravensbrück concentration camp.

56

58

THE NAZI "WELFARE STATE"

The Nazi state appears to take care of everything, from recreation and vacations to art, culture, and health care for mothers and children. This, however, applies only to the *Volksgenossen*, who are racially "pure" and mentally and physically healthy.

60

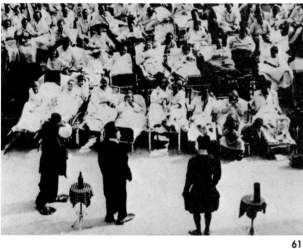

61

62

59, 60, 62 *The Kraft Durch Freude (Strength Through Joy) organization promises vacations and entertainment for every German—a trip to Madeira or Libya, to the mountains to ski or the beach to swim. Kraft Durch Freude arranges vacations for 1 million Germans.*
61 *The famous Fratellini clowns perform for Kraft Durch Freude at the Horst Wessel Hospital.*

The Nazis believe that a healthy nation should not spend money on the mentally disabled, and beginning in October 1939, on Hitler's orders, thousands are quietly killed, with complicated attempts to camouflage what is happening. When news of what is going on leaks out, the German churches voice their indignation over these killings, a stark contrast to their silence about the measures against the Jews. Their protests are effective, and the so-called Euthanasia Project is halted in August 1941. By this time, however, more than 80,000 people have been killed by lethal injection or gas. The figure includes physically or mentally disabled men, women, and children, as well as alcoholics. In the last years of Hitler's dictatorship, another 130,000 patients die of starvation or cold.

63

64

63, 64 *The Nazis try to influence public opinion by publishing photographic comparisons such as these, from the* Little Handbook for Heredity and Race Sciences, *1934. The original caption for photo 63 reads: "A genetically healthy family is forced to live in an old railroad car." For photo 64 it is "Hereditarily mentally handicapped people in an institution."*

65

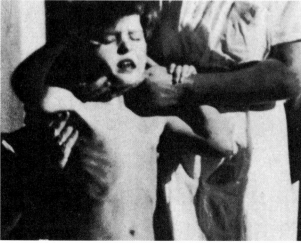

65 *The bodies of more than ten thousand victims are burned in the crematorium at the mental institution in Hadamar.*
66 *A mentally disabled girl is photographed before she is killed.*

The Nazis encourage large families. More children mean more future soldiers, but they must be Aryans—healthy and racially "pure." On June 14, 1933, a law is introduced "to prevent genetically unfit offspring." The result is forced sterilization for individuals who are mentally disabled, epileptic, deaf, or blind.

In September 1935, the Nuremberg laws are passed to "protect German blood and German honor"; they forbid marriage between Jews and non-Jews, and punish Jews and non-Jews who engage in sexual intercourse. In 1937, the Gestapo takes 385 black German children to university hospitals to be sterilized.

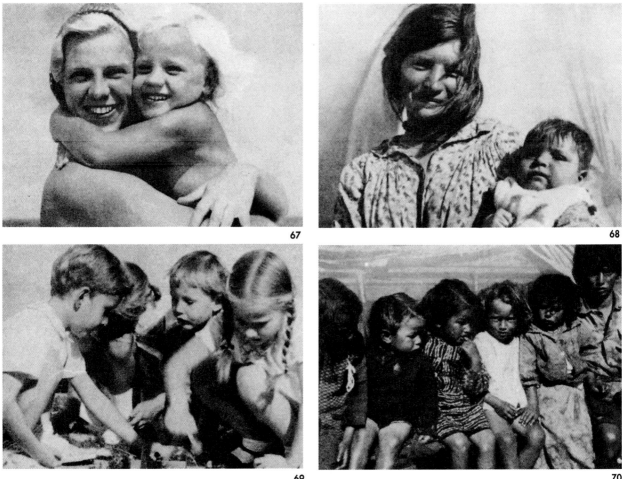

67

68

69

70

67, 68, 69, 70 *"This is how a German mother looks [67], and this is a non-German, alien mother [68]." "These are children of your own blood [69], and these belong to an alien race [70]." From the SS booklet* Victory of Arms, Victory of Children.
71 *The Day of Large Families, Frankfurt, 1937.*

71

The German education system is also brought under Nazi control. On April 7, 1933, a law is passed banning non-Aryans from holding positions as schoolteachers. Hundreds of textbooks are replaced by Nazi publications. New subjects, such as genetics and the study of race and nation, are introduced. In the universities, Jews and political opponents are stripped of their academic titles, and Jews are fired. The number of Jewish and female students is restricted, and in November 1938, Jews are completely barred from ordinary schools and universities. Jewish children can no longer go to school with non-Jewish children. The aim is total segregation.

72 Schoolchildren are taught the Hitler salute.
73 In 1935, Wilhelm Krüger (wearing the traditional academic robe over his Nazi uniform) replaces Eugen Fischer as chancellor of the University of Berlin.
74 In 1942, Sophie Scholl (center) and her brother Hans (right) are active members of a Munich-based resistance organization called the White Rose, but they are captured by the Gestapo and executed after a quick trial. Anti-Nazi student groups such as the White Rose spring up in various German university towns.

73

74

THE YOUTH MOVEMENT

Beginning in 1933, only one youth organization is allowed—the Hitler Youth Movement. Boys join the Hitler Youth; girls join the League of German Girls. The aim is to indoctrinate young people in Nazi ideology, and all other youth organizations are either absorbed or forbidden. For boys the emphasis is on military training, while girls concern themselves with preparing for motherhood. The focus is on sports and physical activities. Reading and other forms of education are considered to be of secondary importance.

76

75 Members of the Hitler Youth salute Hitler in Nuremberg, September 1938.
76, 77 The Hitler Youth Movement and the League of German Girls offer a variety of leisure activities.
78 A League of German Girls sports festival, Frankfurt, 1938.

77

75

78

53

In Hitler's Germany, all arts are made totally subordinate to Nazi ideology. All works of art by Jews and political opponents are either confiscated or destroyed. Architects, sculptors, musicians, painters—even horticulturists—are forced to join Goebbels' "Chamber of Culture."

Hitler promotes naturalist and propagandist painting and dismisses modern art as "crippled paintings." Many artists are forbidden to work because their paintings are declared "degenerate"; the works are either sold abroad or destroyed.

79

79 Artists are forced to choose between leaving Germany, imprisonment, or adapting to the new situation. Film director Leni Riefenstahl (front, center) puts her skills to use for the Nazis. Her famous propaganda movie is Triumph of the Will, a documentary about the Nazi Day of the Party rally in Nuremberg, 1935.

80, 81, 82 The burning of banned books in Berlin, May 10, 1933.

80

81

82

Shortly after coming to power, Hitler meets with the top echelon of the armed forces to discuss his plans. The "shame of Versailles" must be erased. Rearmament, the return of territories lost following World War I, and new "space to live" (*Lebensraum*) in the East are his goals. The armed forces are willing to support Hitler on one condition—limitation of the power of Hitler's paramilitary organization, the SA, whose membership now consists of 2.5 million men. On Hitler's orders, the leaders of the SA are murdered on June 30, 1934, in what is known as the Night of the Long Knives. At the end of 1934, the German army swears its oath of loyalty to Hitler personally. In 1935, the draft is introduced.

83 *General Ludwig Beck resigns in 1938 after learning of Hitler's plan to attack Czechoslovakia. Later, Beck is involved in the attempted murder of Hitler on July 20, 1944. When the attack fails, he commits suicide.*
84 *The first group of new recruits, June 1935.*
85 *Between 1934 and 1939, more than 60 billion German marks are spent on armaments. Only 4 billion marks are made available for social services.*

83

84

85

About half a million Jews are living in Germany in 1933, making up 0.77 percent of the population. Their systematic isolation begins as soon as the Nazis come to power. By April 1933, Jewish civil servants are being dismissed, shopkeepers, doctors, and lawyers are being boycotted, and teachers are losing their jobs. In all aspects of life—work, education, leisure, culture—Jews are separated from non-Jews by a seemingly endless list of decrees. Against all odds, the Jewish community tries to continue normal life as much as possible, though many Jews are now starting to leave the country.

86

86 A farewell—teacher Ruth Ehrmann says goodbye to a pupil who is about to emigrate.

87

88

89

87 The Jewish Cultural Union offers actors and musicians who have been dismissed a chance to continue practicing their professions—but for Jewish audiences only. Photo taken in Grünewald, 1935.
88 Letters provide the only contact with family members and friends who have left the country, 1938.
89 The youth section of Maccabee, the Jewish sports club, 1936.

90, 91 *A carnival float with men dressed as Jews, Cologne, 1934. The signs in photo 91 read "The last ones disappear. We're only on a short trip to Liechtenstein and Jaffa."*

90

91

92

92 *"Away to Dachau"—
a carnival float with men
in concentration camp
uniforms, Nuremberg, 1936.*
93 *Puppets wearing the Star
of David hang from mock
gallows in the Nuremberg
carnival, 1938.*

93

KRISTALLNACHT

Beginning on November 9, 1938, and over the next few days, scores of synagogues and thousands of Jewish-owned shops all over Germany and Austria are ransacked and burned. The event becomes known as Kristallnacht, or "Night of Broken Glass," after the windows shattered in the rampage.

The first mass arrests of Jews take place on November 12. About 30,000 Jewish men and boys are seized and deported to the Buchenwald, Dachau, and Sachsenhausen concentration camps. Kristallnacht marks the stepping up of the persecution of the Jews.

94 *The shattered windows of Jewish shops, November 1938.*
95 *Frankfurt's synagogue on fire, Börneplatz, November 9, 1938.*
96 *Burning the synagogue's furniture in Tiengen, November 10, 1938.*

94

95

96

JEWISH REFUGEES

Jews have been leaving Germany in increasing numbers since 1933, but Kristallnacht triggers a mass exodus, and by the spring of 1939, around half of the country's Jewish population has fled.

The problem for Jewish refugees is where to go—they are not welcome everywhere. Many countries rapidly place a quota on the number of Jews they allow to enter. In some cases, countries even close their borders. As a result, German Jewish refugees are scattered throughout the world, sometimes reaching their destinations through bizarre and roundabout routes.

97

97 A travel agency on Meinekestrasse, Berlin, 1939.
98 These girls are on their way to Britain.
99 From 1938 onward, many Jewish parents in Germany and Austria send their children to other countries, in the hope that they will be safer there.
100 The arrival of Jewish refugees in Shanghai, China. By 1940, about 20,000 Jews have been allowed to settle there.

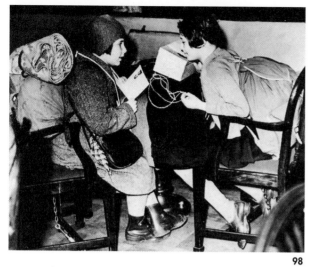

98

99

100

The reactions of other countries to the Nazi regime differ markedly. Some strongly oppose the developments in Germany. Others do not believe Hitler will hold on to power for long and do not want to get involved. Still others are so enthusiastic about Hitler that they organize Nazi movements at home. In general, the dangers of National Socialism and the persecution of the Jews are underestimated.

102

101 *In 1933 eighteen-year-old Sara Roth chains herself to a streetlamp in Washington, D.C., in protest against the mass arrests of socialists and communists in Germany.*
102 *In London, November 1938, a plea to open Palestine to Jewish refugees.*
103 *A branch of the SA is formed in California. Organizations sympathetic to the Nazis are founded in a number of countries.*

103

68

Following Hitler's rise to power and after the anti-Jewish boycott, Otto Frank leaves Frankfurt for Amsterdam in 1933. He starts a Dutch branch of the Opekta Company there, manufacturing products used in jam making, such as pectin. Soon Edith, Margot, and Anne join him.

The Frank family moves into a house on Merwedeplein in the southern part of the city. The girls attend the Montessori school nearby and make lots of friends—photographs document their many outings. The family also becomes close friends with other Jewish immigrants who settle in their neighborhood. The Opekta Company is doing rather well.

104

105

104, 105 *Anne with her friend Sanne Ledermann in 1935, on Merwedeplein, Amsterdam.*
106, 107 *Summer 1934.*
108 *Anne (right) with a friend, 1934.*

106

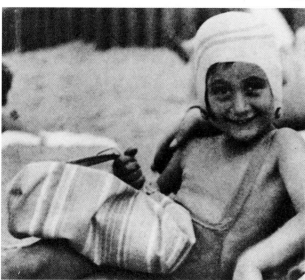

107

108

109 *Anne (arrowed) at her Montessori school, 1935.*
110 *In Amstelrust Park with a rabbit, 1938.*

109

110

111

112

113

111 Anne (second from the left) on her tenth birthday, June 12, 1939.
112 Anne.
113 Anne (right) with Margot (left) and a friend (also called Margot) on the beach at Middelkerke, Belgium, July 1937.

114

115

114 *Anne on the roof of the house on Merwedeplein, 1940.*
115 *The Frank family on Merwedeplein, May 1940.*
116 *Anne with friends Hermann and Herbert Wilp.*

116

117 *Margot (left) and
Anne, 1940.*
118 *On the beach in
Zandvoort, August 1940.*
119 *Anne, 1940.*

1935

1935

1936

1937

1938

1939

1940

1941

1942

121 *Anne.*

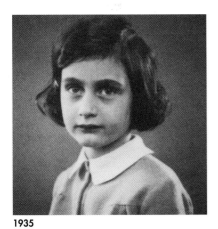

1935

1935

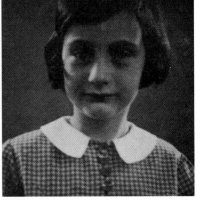

1936

1937

1938

1939

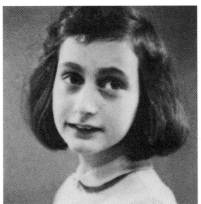

1940

1941

1942

In 1931, Anton Mussert founds the National Socialist Movement (NSB) in the Netherlands, modeled on the German Nazi Party. The party grows quickly at first, attracting a following of businessmen, civil servants, and farmers who have lost faith in the country's mainstream political parties. In 1935, the NSB captures nearly 8 percent of the vote. After 1935, however, its popularity diminishes, partly because of its anti-Semitism.

124

122 Anton Mussert, leader of the NSB.
123 NSB sympathizers.
124 An NSB rally.
125 "Moscow threatens! Vote Mussert!" The NSB is fiercely anticommunist in the election campaign.
126 An NSB propaganda van carries the slogan "Fascism means action for people and fatherland."

125

123

126

In 1940, the Jewish population of the Netherlands is about 140,000, of whom around 24,000 are refugees. The Dutch government is not convinced of the Jews' need to flee from Germany, and restricts the number of immigrants. The only assistance available is provided by refugee camps such as Westerbork, for which the Dutch Jewish community has to supply all the funding.

With 90,000 Jews, Amsterdam has the largest Jewish population. Most are poor and work in shops or in the garment and diamond industries. Although there are expressions of anti-Semitism, most Jews in the Netherlands feel they have become part of the Dutch community.

127

127 *A house on Uilenburg, a street in Amsterdam's Jewish quarter.*
128 *A matzo bakery in Amsterdam's Jewish quarter.*
129 *The Waterlooplein market, in the center of Amsterdam's Jewish quarter.*
130 *Jews at work in the diamond industry.*

128

129

130

The German invasion begins on May 10, 1940, and takes the Netherlands completely by surprise. The country had expected to remain neutral, as it had done during World War I.

The Germans move swiftly, seizing key areas within a few days. The prime minister and his cabinet, as well as the royal family, fly to England. After fierce fighting near Arnhem and the bombing of Rotterdam, the Netherlands is forced to surrender. As of May 15, 1940, the country is under German occupation.

132

133

131 German paratroopers land in the Netherlands, May 10, 1940.
132, 133 More than 900 people are killed and more than 24,000 houses are destroyed during the bombing of Rotterdam.
134 Dutch soldiers surrender their weapons at the Binnenhof, the seat of government in The Hague.

134

After the initial shock and terror of the invasion, most Dutch citizens are relieved that the Germans are behaving "properly." The majority do not question the Germans' right to impose new laws. Some measures, such as blackouts, seem reasonable. Others, such as the introduction of the ID card, are bearable. In the face of Germany's apparent invincibility, it seems sensible to adapt to the inevitable.

From the autumn of 1940 onward, the majority of Jewish and non-Jewish civil servants, employers, teachers, and judges fill out the "Declaration of Aryanism," stating whether or not they or their personnel's parents and grandparents are Jewish. Compliance with this request is virtually total; in the whole country there are only a few dozen refusals to fill in the form. This widespread Dutch obedience provides the German authorities with crucial information that makes the persecution of Dutch Jews an easy next step.

135

137

136

138

135 Issuing ration cards, which are needed to buy food.

136 Voting booths in Rotterdam are converted into changing rooms for a swimming pool.

137 Railings are erected alongside canals in Amsterdam because the blackout makes walking at night dangerous.

138 As of May 1941, every Dutch citizen is required to carry an ID card—a first for the Netherlands. Shown here, the registration in Amsterdam.

84

That the Germans mean business becomes clear in February 1941. The NSB's paramilitary arm, the Weer Afdeling (WA), repeatedly enters Amsterdam's Jewish quarter, acting in an aggressive and brutal manner. Markets on Waterlooplein and at Amstelveld are raided.

Amsterdam's Jews organize groups to defend their property. Heavy fighting ensues. When a WA man dies, the Germans retaliate. On February 22, the Jewish quarter is sealed off and 400 Jewish men and boys are rounded up from the streets, homes, and coffeehouses. They are beaten and taken away—where, no one knows.

THE FEBRUARY STRIKE, 1941

To protest against this roundup, a general strike is organized immediately, led chiefly by the Communist Party. Tens of thousands take part, in and around Amsterdam. On the second day, the Germans retaliate with force, sending in troops to restore order. Shots are fired. People are arrested. In fear of further reprisals, the strike ends on February 27, 1941.

Wij ontvingen heden het droeve bericht, dat onze geliefde Zoon, Broeder en Kleinzoon

ARNOLD HEILBUT,

in den leeftijd van 18 jaar, in Duitschland is overleden.

Amsterdam, 2 Juli 1941.
Z. Amstellaan 89.

H. M. HEILBUT.
F. HEILBUT—CARO
en familie.

Heden ontvingen wij bericht, dat in Duitschland op 25 Juni is overleden onze innig geliefde Zoon, Broeder en Zwager

AB. LOPES DE LEAô LAGUNA,

in den leeftijd van 24 jaar.
Namens de familie:

B. LOPES DE LEAô
LAGUNA.

Verzoeke geen bezoek.
Smaragdstraat 25 I Z.

Met diep leedwezen geven wij kennis, dat onze innig geliefde eenige Zoon

PAUL JACOBUS LEO,

in den ouderdom van 27 jaar, 25 Juni in Duitschland is overleden.

I. HEIMANS JR.
J. B. HEIMANS—
VAN GELDER.

Amsterdam, 1 Juli 1941.
Watteaustraat 5.

Liever geen rouwbeklag.

142

141 Streetcar drivers on strike in Sarphati Street.
142 Several months after the February roundup, relatives of the arrested Jews are sent death notices from Mauthausen concentration camp.

The Dutch National Socialist organizations, of which the NSB is the largest, cooperate with the Germans. They arrange rallies to demonstrate their anti-Semitic and pro-Nazi attitudes. Other collaborators include those hoping to profit from the occupation in various ways, ranging from selling cakes to the German army to building military installations.

143 *Arthur Seyss-Inquart is appointed Reich commissioner of the Netherlands by Hitler in 1940. Here Seyss-Inquart (center) and Anton Mussert (in black) inspect German troops at the Binnenhof, The Hague.*
144 *"With Adolf Hitler into a new Europe," at the NSB rally in Museumplein, Amsterdam, June 27, 1941. Here Mussert claims: "The German people can count on us as their most loyal guardian."*
145 *The smashed windows of the New Israelite Weekly, 1941.*

89

144

143

145

The Germans solicit volunteers for the war in Eastern Europe by appealing to deep-rooted anticommunist feelings. No fewer than 30,000 Dutch men and boys offer their services to the Waffen SS (the military SS corps), of which 17,000 are admitted beginning in April 1941. Another 15,000 volunteer for police groups and military auxiliary organizations.

146

148

149

146 *General Seyffardt inspects Dutch volunteers before their departure for the Russian front, The Hague, August 7, 1941.*
147 *Female members of the NSB knit clothes for volunteers at the Russian front.*
148 *Volunteers departing for the Russian front, The Hague, July 1941.*
149 *Anton Mussert (left) visiting a training camp of Dutch Nazi volunteers in East Prussia.*

147

ANTI-JEWISH MEASURES

Throughout 1941, the Jewish community becomes increasingly isolated as, step by step, the rights of Jews are restricted. The separation of Jews from non-Jews is the first aim of the German authorities. In February 1941, all Jewish teachers are dismissed from mainstream schools, and starting in September 1941, Jewish children are banned from these as well and have to attend special Jewish schools. In 1941 and 1942, a series of anti-Jewish measures are implemented, just as happened in Germany between 1933 and 1938. Jews are forbidden from entering all public places such as parks, swimming pools, cinemas, markets, and shops, and a Jewish ghetto is established in the center of Amsterdam. Starting at the end of April 1942, all Jews have to wear a yellow cotton Star of David, bearing the word *Jood*, on their clothes.

The Germans force prominent Jews to form a council to represent all Jews. The Jewish leaders agree to do this in the hope of avoiding a worse alternative. The Jewish Council in Amsterdam continues to work for its community for two years, organizing schools and teachers for Jewish children, providing social workers, and arranging cultural activities. The Germans use the Jewish Council as a means of executing their orders, especially once the deportations of Jews begin.

150 The sign in this grocery store window reads "Jews not allowed."

151 By February 1943, most of the shops in the Jewish quarter have been shut down by the Germans as part of the Aryanization program introduced in 1941.

152 Jewish ID cards are stamped with a J, summer 1941.

153 Another "Jews not allowed" sign, this time at a swimming pool.

152

153

155

154 *Jewish teenagers at Transvaalplein, Amsterdam, spring 1942. Many Jewish people live in the Transvaal quarter.*

155 *Having been fired from their jobs, Jewish musicians are allowed to perform only in Jewish homes.*

156 *The sign on the door behind this Jewish couple— Mr. and Mrs. Peereboom— reads "Stars sold out." Jews were responsible not only for wearing the yellow stars, but for buying them too.*

154

156

DUTCH RESISTANCE

Although the Dutch dislike German occupation, they are ill prepared to form a resistance movement, and only a tiny minority of the population actively opposes the Nazis. Many factors immobilize the Dutch—fear, religious principles, a fundamental distaste for civil disobedience, and the view that a choice needs to be made between fascism and communism.

The coordination of the Dutch resistance is hampered by political and religious differences, especially in the first year of the German occupation. No clear example of opposition is set by leading circles in Dutch society either.

The Nederlandsche Unie (Dutch Union, or NU) is founded as a form of anti-German protest and attracts more than a million members in under a year. Looking for ways to cooperate with the German authorities and thereby keep their independence, the NU leaders are willing to comply with some measures taken, although they protest against the anti-Jewish decrees. The NU is banned by the German authorities in 1941.

It isn't until 1942–1943 that a more efficient resistance movement develops.

157

158

157, 158, 159 *Setting up an underground press is a key resistance activity. About 30,000 people are involved in listening to the Allied radio stations, then spreading the information through stenciled or printed bulletins.*

159

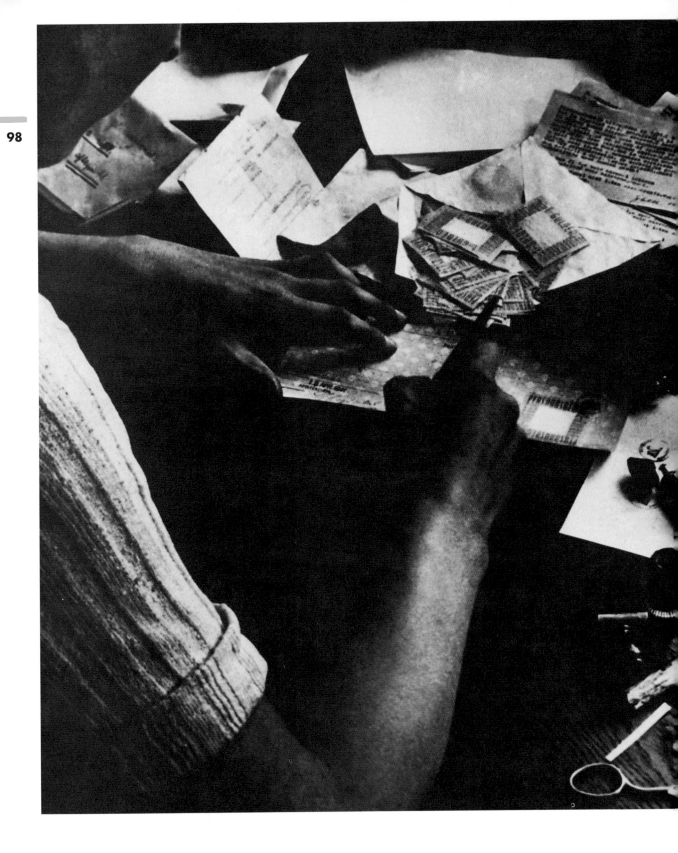

160 False identity cards are created, 1942.
161 Files from the town of Jisp's registration office are hidden from the Nazis in a barn.

162 Amsterdam's registration office, where vital population statistics are kept, is demolished by a resistance group.

161

160

162

Starting in January 1942, unemployed Jewish men are called upon to report for work in the eastern Netherlands. The next step is to summon not just the men but their entire families to the Westerbork camp, which now serves as a transit center from where, beginning in July 1942, the men and their families are deported to "labor camps" in the East.

Thousands try to hide, but it is very difficult to find a place of safety. The Nazis put pressure on the Jewish Council to deliver specific numbers of people to Westerbork. When the quotas are not met, Jews are arrested at random. Those who work for the council are omitted from the deportation lists—for a while. The leaders and staff of the Jewish Council are themselves arrested and deported from Westerbork in September 1943.

164

163 *Only a few Jews are able to find a hiding place. These Jewish children have been taken in at the Boogaard family's farm.*
164 *A roundup of men forced to work in Germany, The Hague, November 1944.*

Formally, Otto Frank "Aryanizes" his business, but he remains in charge behind the scenes. Until the summer holidays of 1942, Anne and Margot attend the Jewish Lyceum, a school for Jewish children banned from other schools.

In 1941, the Franks begin preparations to go into hiding. Thanks to the help of his staff at the Opekta Company (Victor Kugler, Johannes Kleiman, Miep Gies, and Bep Voskuijl), Otto Frank is able to prepare a secret place for his own family and that of another employee, Hermann van Pels, in the two upper floors of the old building his firm occupies.

On July 5, 1942, Margot Frank receives a notice to report to a "labor camp." The Franks move into what they call the Secret Annex—concealed behind a movable bookcase—at 263 Prinsengracht the following day. One week later, they are joined by Mr. and Mrs. van Pels and their son, Peter, and finally, in November, by Fritz Pfeffer, a dentist.

In her diary, given to her by her father on her thirteenth birthday, June 12, 1942, Anne Frank movingly records the experiences of everyday life in hiding. After a while she decides to write her diary entries in the form of letters addressed to "Kitty"—a character in a novel she has enjoyed. Later, after hearing a radio broadcast saying that letters and diaries about life under German occupation might be published after the war, Anne decides to edit and revise her diary. She makes it more like a novel, changing the names of her "characters." Kugler and Kleiman become Kraler and Koophuis, the van Pelses become the van Daans, Pfeffer becomes Dussel, Bep Voskuijl becomes Elli Vossen, and Miep Gies becomes Anne van Santen.

166

165 The Secret Annex (at the top of the central building).

166 The eight people in hiding (from left to right, top to bottom): Otto, Edith, Anne, and Margot Frank; Hermann and Auguste van Pels and their son, Peter; Fritz Pfeffer.

167 The helpers of the people in hiding (from left to right): Johannes Kleiman, Miep Gies, Bep Voskuijl, and Victor Kugler.

167

168 *Anne Frank's room. Her diary entry for July 11, 1942, reads: "Up till now our bedroom, with its blank walls, was very bare. Thanks to Father—who brought my entire postcard and film-star collection here beforehand— and to a brush and a pot of glue, I was able to plaster the walls with pictures. It looks much more cheerful."*

169 *On August 21, 1942, Anne writes: "Now our Secret Annex has truly become secret. Because so many houses are being searched for hidden bicycles, Mr. Kugler thought it would be better to have a bookcase built in front of the entrance to our hiding place. It swings out on its hinges and opens like a door. Mr. Voskuijl did the carpentry work. (Mr. Voskuijl has been told that the seven of us are in hiding, and he's been most helpful.)" In this photo, Johannes Kleiman is standing next to the bookcase.*

170 *The attic, where Anne usually writes in her diary.*

168

169

172

171 A present-day aerial view of Prinsengracht, Westerkerk, and the Secret Annex. On July 11, 1942, Anne writes: "Father, Mother, and Margot still can't get used to the chiming of the Westertoren clock, which tells us the time every quarter of an hour. Not me, I liked it from the start; it sounds so reassuring, especially at night."

172 A page from Anne's diary.

173

173 Anne. On December 24, 1943, she writes: "Believe me, if you've been shut up for a year and a half, it can get to be too much for you sometimes. But feelings can't be ignored, no matter how unjust or ungrateful they seem. I long to ride a bike, dance, whistle, look at the world, feel young and know that I'm free, and yet I can't let it show. Just imagine what would happen if all eight of us were to feel sorry for ourselves or walk around with the discontent clearly visible on our faces. Where would that get us?"

In the autumn of 1942, the German military loses ground. This, together with the Allied advances in North Africa, the Russian counterattack, and the fall of Mussolini, inspires the Dutch resistance movement. At the same time, however, the Nazi repression of the Dutch people is stepped up. From the summer of 1944 onward, hundreds of resistance fighters are executed.
In September 1944, the total number of Dutch citizens is about 9 million. Around 250,000 of the non-Jewish population are in hiding, 12,500 are prisoners of war, 7,000 are political prisoners, and 300,000 are working as forced laborers. Another 900,000 have left their homes to escape being sent to Germany for forced labor.

174

174 A traitor's death.
Resistance groups hold
emotional discussions on
whether they have the right
to execute traitors.
175 In 1943–1944, tens of
thousands of men are forced
to go to Germany to work.
176 Many men and young
people go into hiding, mostly
on farms, to escape being
sent to Germany.

175

110

In 1943, one transport of deported Jews follows another until Westerbork is full and life becomes unbearable. The majority stay at the transit camp for several weeks, some more than a year. From there they are shipped in weekly transports to the extermination camps in Poland—Auschwitz, Birkenau, and Sobibor in particular. Later transports go to Bergen-Belsen and Theresienstadt in Germany.

Meanwhile, everyone tries to avoid deportation by getting exemption stamps in their identification papers. Some Jewish families are able to obtain passports from other countries and save themselves that way. Others try to prove their families were baptized generations before. The possibilities are extremely limited, as most escape routes are closed. For those without an exemption stamp, each night becomes a torment because of the police roundups. Deportations from the Netherlands continue until September 1944. Deportation means almost certain death.

177

177 *Waiting to be sent to Westerbork, the Dutch transit camp. The photograph was taken for an SS magazine in Amsterdam, May 26, 1943.*
178 *Jews leave Amsterdam's Muiderpoort Station for Westerbork.*
179 *Arriving at Westerbork.*

178

179

THE FINAL SOLUTION

In 1941, Nazi leaders make the decision "to cleanse Europe of Jews." As the German army marches through Eastern Europe, it is followed by special SS units called *Einsatzgruppen*, which begin the mass execution of Jews. More than 1 million are shot. The Wannsee Conference, held in a suburb of Berlin on January 20, 1942, under the leadership of Adolf Eichmann, finalizes plans for the annihilation of Europe's 11 million Jews and others, drawing on the Nazis' experience of gassing already obtained from killing the disabled.

The plans become known as the *Endlösung,* the Final Solution of the "Jewish question." Extermination and labor camps are built. A large number of the deported Jews—mostly mothers, children, and the elderly—are gassed on arrival. The remainder are forced to work until they die of exhaustion, starvation, or disease. Nearly 6 million Jews die in the camps.

Countless other people also die in Nazi concentration camps—Poles, political opponents, homosexuals, Jehovah's Witnesses, "antisocial elements," Russian prisoners of war, and several hundred thousand Gypsies.

180

180 *Dutch Jews departing from Westerbork transit camp for Auschwitz, one of the largest extermination camps, in southwest Poland.*
181 *Jews in Eastern Europe are rounded up by Einsatzgruppen (special SS units) and murdered.*

181

182

183

184

185

182 When Hungarian Jews arrive at Auschwitz, they are divided into two groups—those who are able to work and those intended for immediate extermination. (The tall officer at the right of the picture is the infamous Josef Mengele.)

183 IG Farben, a large chemical cartel, operates an enormous factory near Auschwitz. The death toll among forced laborers at the factory is extremely high.

184 A number is tattooed on the arms of those who survive the selection process on arrival at the camps. This Gypsy woman is one of the few survivors.

185 Guards at Dachau concentration camp. Dachau was originally for communists and political prisoners but later was used for Jewish men.

116

On June 6, 1944—D-Day—the Allies in the West (Britain and the Commonwealth, especially Canada; the United States; and various free forces from the occupied countries) land on the Normandy beaches. On August 25, Paris falls to the Allies; on September 4, they take Brussels; on September 5 (Wild Tuesday), they arrive in the Netherlands, although it will be many months more before the country is completely liberated. The German forces resist strongly, but the Allies enter Germany at Aachen in October 1944 and cross the Rhine in March 1945. Meanwhile, in Eastern Europe the Soviet Red Army moves westward toward Germany. The Western Allied forces join up with their Eastern counterpart, the Red Army, in Berlin, which falls.

186

187

188

186 The D-Day landings, June 6, 1944.
187 NSB members hurry to leave the Netherlands on Wild Tuesday, September 5, 1944. Photo taken at The Hague railway station.
188 The village of Rijswijk waits in vain for Allied troops to arrive on Wild Tuesday.
189 Allied soldiers hand out chewing gum in the Netherlands' liberated south.

189

On August 4, 1944, the Secret Annex is raided by SS sergeant Karl Josef Silberbauer, with several Dutch Nazis. All eight Jews in hiding and two of their helpers, Victor Kugler and Johannes Kleiman, are arrested.

Kugler and Kleiman are taken to a remand prison. Kleiman is released on September 18 after intervention by the Red Cross. Kugler is part of a forced march to a labor camp in Germany in March 1945, but manages to escape and make his way back to Amsterdam.

The Franks, the van Pelses, and Fritz Pfeffer are taken to Westerbork transit camp. They are all put on the final train that leaves for Auschwitz on September 3, 1944.

Mr. van Pels dies in the gas chamber at Auschwitz in October or November 1944. At the end of October 1944, Margot and Anne Frank are transported to the disease-ridden Bergen-Belsen camp in Germany. Fritz Pfeffer is transported to Neuengamme concentration camp, where he dies on December 20, 1944. Edith Frank dies of hunger and exhaustion in Auschwitz on January 6, 1945. Both Margot and Anne contract typhoid and die in Bergen-Belsen in March 1945. Mrs. van Pels is also moved to Bergen-Belsen and from there to Theresienstadt, where she dies in April 1945. When Auschwitz is abandoned because of the approaching Russian army, Peter van Pels is sent to Mauthausen in Austria, where he dies on May 5, 1945, three days before the camp is liberated.

Otto Frank is the only one from the Secret Annex to survive the camps. He is freed from Auschwitz by Russian troops on January 27, 1945.

190 *The destination sign on the Westerbork-Auschwitz train.*
191 *The Frank family's names in the list of Jewish deportees on the last Westerbork-Auschwitz train, September 3, 1944. The train leaves just two days before the Allies reach the Netherlands.*

190

JUDENTRANSPORT AUS DEN NIEDERLANDEN – LAGER WESTERBORK

Haeftlinge

```
301. ✓Engers          Isidor — ✓30.4. 93 — Kaufmann
302✓ Engers           Leonard  15.6. 20 — Lamdarbeiter
303✓ Franco           Manfred — ✓1.5.  05 — Verleger
304. Frank            Arthur   22.8. 81   Kaufmann
305. Frank ✗          Isaac   ✓29.11.87   Installateur
306. Frank            Margot   16.2. 26   ohne
307. Frank       ✓    Otto    ✓12.5. 89   Kaufmann
308.✓ Frank-Hollaender Edith   16.1. 00   ohne
309. Frank            Anneliese 12.6. 29  ohne
310. v.Franck         Sara —   27.4. 02 — Typistin
311. Franken          Rozanna  16.5. 96 — Landarbeiter
312.✓Franken-Weyand   Johanna  24.12.96✓ Landbauer
313. Franken          Hermann — ✓12.5.34  ohne
314. Franken          Louis    10.8. 17 — Gaertner
315. Franken ℜ        Rosalina 29.3. 27   Landbau
316. Frankfort        Alex     14.11.19 — Dr.i.d.Oekonomie
317. Frankfort-Elsas  Regina   11.12.19   Apoth-.Ass.
318. Frankfoort ✗     Elias   ✓22.10.98 — Schneider
319.✓Frankfort ℜ      Max      20.6. 21   Schneider
320.✓Frankfort-Weijl ℜ Hetty   29.3. 24   Naeherin
321.✓Frankfort-WerkendamℜRosette 24.6.98  Schriftstellerin
322.✓Frijda           Hermann  22.6. 87 — Hochschullehrer
323. Frenk            Henriette 28.4. 21  Typistin
324. Frenk ℜ          Rosa     15.3.24    Haushalthilfe
325. Friezer          Isaac    10.3. 20 — Korrespondent
326.✓Fruitman-Vlessche-
          dragerℜFanny          24.1. 03   ohne
327. Gans ✗           Elie    ✓24.10.03 — Betriebleiter
328. Gans-Koopman ℜ   Gesina   20.12.05   Maschinestrickeri
329. Gans             Kalman — 6.3.  79   Diamantarbeiter
330. Gans ℜ           Klara    12.5. 13   Naeherin
331. Gans ·           Paul —   27.9. 08 — Landbauer
332. v.Gelder         Abraham — 9.11.78   Metzger
333. v.Gelder-de Jong Reintje  22.10.81   ohne
334. v.Gelder         Alexander 27.6. 03 — Kaufmann
```

Though the Allies reach the Netherlands in September 1944, they fail to liberate the entire country.

The Dutch government in exile in London orders a railway strike, hoping to break Germany's hold on the country. The Germans retaliate by forbidding food deliveries to Dutch cities. The enormous shortages that follow are made worse when the Germans begin confiscating food. When deliveries of coal and other fuel to the cities are also halted, the situation becomes critical. Everything burnable is used for heat. Everything edible is eaten, even tulip bulbs. Thousands of children are sent to the countryside to be fed. As many as 22,000 people die of hunger. Tens of thousands are seriously ill. Meanwhile, the Germans take anything of value from the Netherlands and send it to Germany—from cattle to bicycles, machines, factory equipment, and trains.

193

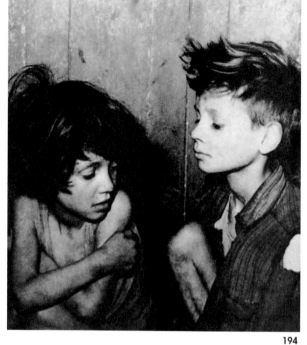

194

195

192 Children take an old door home for firewood.
193 People demolish their own homes to obtain wood for fuel.
194 Starving children.
195 In the countryside, thousands of people try to exchange goods for food.

122

As the Soviet Red Army moves toward Germany from the east and the Western Allies close in from the west at the beginning of 1945, the Nazis try to evacuate the extermination camps in an attempt to conceal what has been happening there.

Under its leader, General Georgy Zhukov, the Red Army enters and liberates Auschwitz on January 27, 1945. As the camps in Poland fall to the Russians, the Nazis make prisoners march through snow and rain toward Germany. Hundreds of thousands are forced to join this march, and huge numbers die on the way; in Germany the camps become overfull and even more unsanitary. Heinrich Himmler, in charge of the camps, even tries to issue official orders to stop the extermination program, presumably as an insurance policy to save his own skin.

What the Allies find as they reach and liberate the camps is indescribable—appalling scenes of death, starvation, and disease. A difficult journey home begins for the survivors, and the homecoming is a bitter disappointment for many. Most have lost their family and friends. Their houses are occupied. Their property has been stolen. Many survivors encounter ignorance and disbelief about their experiences. Only 4,700 of the 110,000 Dutch Jews who were deported return from the camps.

197

196 Dachau is liberated by U.S. troops, April 30, 1945.
197 After the liberation of Bergen-Belsen, the camp where Anne and Margot Frank died in March 1945, the barracks are set on fire to halt the spread of typhoid fever, April 1945.
198 Temporary repatriation camps are set up in hotels and schools.

198

In April 1945, British planes drop food over the starving Netherlands, ensuring the survival of thousands of people. A few weeks later, the war is over and the remainder of the country is liberated by the Allied forces. As the nation celebrates, the Nazis and their collaborators are arrested. More than 75 percent of the Netherlands' Jewish population—over 100,000 people—have been killed during the war. Of the 24,000 Jews who found hiding places, 16,000 survive. The other 8,000 Jews were betrayed or otherwise discovered, deported, and killed. May and June 1945 are months of liberation and festivities but also a time of desperate waiting and looking for missing family members and friends.

199 British bombers loaded
with parcels of food fly over
Rotterdam, April 30, 1945.
200 Liberation celebrations
in Amsterdam.

125

During the final months of the war, Germany is subjected to extremely heavy bombing, which proves to be a major factor in the move toward surrender. Hitler shoots himself in Berlin on April 30, 1945. On the following day, Goebbels shoots first his wife and then himself, having already poisoned their six children. Many senior Nazis are eventually arrested and tried, though some escape. Admiral Karl Dönitz, whom Hitler named as his successor, surrenders, and the capitulation is signed on May 7, after which Germany comes under the joint control of the Allies—Russian, American, British, and other troops.

In the Far East the war goes on until Japan surrenders on August 14, 1945, after the dropping of atomic bombs on Hiroshima and Nagasaki.

201

201 An American placard welcomes the Russians to Germany.
202 American and Russian soldiers meet at the Elbe River, Germany.
203 Frankfurt in ruins.
204 Jewish survivors, liberated from Theresienstadt concentration camp in Bohemia (now the Czech Republic), return to Frankfurt.
205 These young boys are members of the Hitler Youth, arrested with other German soldiers.

203

202

204

205

On his way back to Amsterdam, where he arrives on June 3, 1945, Otto Frank learns that his wife is dead. It takes longer to find out what has happened to his daughters. When the news comes that Anne and Margot are dead, Miep Gies gives him Anne's diary, which she rescued after the Secret Annex was raided. She had hoped to return it to Anne one day. Friends persuade Otto Frank to publish Anne's diary, and it first appears in 1947 under the title *Het Achterhuis* (The Annex). To date, the diary has been translated into more than 55 different languages, and more than 25 million copies have been sold around the world.

The house at 263 Prinsengracht where Anne and the others lived in hiding is now a museum, operated by the Anne Frank House, founded in 1957. As well as preserving the Annex, the Anne Frank House tries to stimulate the fight against anti-Semitism, racism, and fascism through educational projects and the spread of information.

206 *On November 10, 1953, Otto Frank remarries in Amsterdam. His new wife is Elfriede Geiringer from Vienna, who also survived Auschwitz and lost her son and husband in the concentration camps. Otto Frank dies in Switzerland on August 19, 1980, at the age of ninety-one.*

207 *Otto Frank advertises for information about the whereabouts of his daughters, Margot and Anne, in the Dutch newspaper Het Vrije Volk (The Free People), August 1, 1945.*

208 *The cover of the first Dutch edition of Anne's diary.*

209 *Miep Gies (second from left) and her husband, Jan, show British schoolchildren one of the rooms in the Secret Annex, May 1987. The children have won a drawing competition about discrimination.*

206

JET CITROEN, geb. '99, LIES CITROEN, geb '05, die gezamelijk 2 Sept. 1944 van Westerbork naar Auschwitz gevoerd zijn. J. J. MAARSEN, De Clercqstraat 148, Haarlem.

WILLEM TOON DEIJNS en JAN MULDER, won. te A'dam, waarsch. werkz. bij P.T.T., zo spoedig mogelijk inl. versch. over BAS MEINDERS, heeft gewerkt bij R.P.D. te Berlijn. Lager Greifwalderstrasse 34—35. Zij hebben nog papieren van hem in hun bezit, Mevr. de Wed. C. MEINDERS—BECK, Aliard Piersonlaan 133, Den Haag. Alle onk. worden gaarne vergoed.

ROSA SOPERSTEIN, geb. 19 Dec. 1919, uit Westerbork vertr. Sept. 1943 met transport Joodse Raad? ANNIE SPANJAART, Transvaalkade 92 b, A'dam-O.

CARLA ROSE LEVY, geb. 1 Juli 1917; 11 Mei 1943 van Westerbork naar Polen gedeporteerd. Mr. ALFRED LEVY, Westeinde 22 A'dam, tel. 34593.

Onze ouders MOZES GROEN geb. 2-7-1892, doorgez. van Westerbork eind Oct. 1942 naar? En KEETJE GROEN—ROOSELAAR geb. 24-6-1897, opgep. 29-3-'44 sindsdiens niets bekend. N. Groen p.a. I. Fieseler, Kastanjeweg 9 II.

J. W. GERRITSEN, geb. 10-7-'06 te Deventer gearr. 22 Mei '44 te Groningen, 27 Mei '44 naar Arnhem en 10 Juni '44 naar Amersfoort tot Oct. '44 en vermoedelijk naar Buchenwalde of Neuengamme vervoerd. A. BOSCH, Soembawastr. 49 hs. of mevr. L. GERRITSEN—STRAALMAN, Jan Steenstr. 27, Deventer.

LOUIS VOORSANGER, geb. 5-12-'85, vertrokk. Westerbork 18 Mei '43 n. Duitsland. E. Auerhaan, Pieter Aertszstr. 119 III.

IRMA SPIELMANN, geb. 10-4-'94 Wenen, Tsj. Slow. nation. Weggevoerd Westerborg 23-3-'43. Wie weet iets van dit transport? Spielmann, Scheldestr. 181 III, Zuid.

MARGOT FRANK (19 j.) en ANNA FRANK (16 j.), in Jan. op transp. vanuit Bergen-Belzen. O. Frank, Prinsengracht 263, tel. 37059.

Mijn man ALFRED v. GELDEREN (Oct. 1942 uit Westerb.) en kinderen DORA ROSA en FREDERIK MARTHIJN (24-7-1942 uit Westerb.) Marianne v. Gelderen—Engelander, Jozef Israelkade 126 II.

FRANCISCUS JOHANNES MAAS geb. 19-10-'23, werkz. bij Machinefabriek Winger en Co. Waltersdorf Kreis Zittau Saksen Duitsland. Inl. gevr. van hen, die hem na 16 Sept. 1944 hebben gezien. J. Ch.

207

208

209

Anti-Semitism was not a Nazi invention, and it did not disappear with the collapse of the Third Reich. Old prejudices against the Jews are again coming to the surface, and anti-Semitism is expressed by diverse social groups in many countries. Today, anti-Semitic reading matter is openly being sold, especially in Eastern Europe and in several Middle Eastern countries, and is also widely available through the Internet.

Groups of neo-Nazis around the world have continued to keep Nazi ideology alive, even denying that the persecution of the Jews ever took place. Some postwar Nazis attach themselves to political parties, refraining from using Nazi terminology openly because it would scare off voters. Others intentionally use Nazi symbols to provoke media attention and try to spread doubt about the basic facts of the Holocaust.

210 Neo-Nazis demonstrating in the center of Berlin in support of Jörg Haider, the Austrian leader of the right-wing extremist Freedom Party, March 2000.

211 On July 18, 1994, 86 people die and hundreds more are injured during the bombing of a Jewish social service center in Buenos Aires, Argentina.

212 In September 1990, 4,000 inhabitants of Ihringen hold a silent demonstration at the desecrated Jewish cemetery in Baden-Württemberg, Germany.

213 In April 2000, the British writer David Irving loses a libel case against American historian Deborah Lipstadt, who called him a Holocaust denier.

211

213

212

Although it is a long-established scientific fact that human beings are a single species, *Homo sapiens,* there have always been people who divide humanity up into "races" and claim that one race is better than another. In the United States and Canada, the Ku Klux Klan, which emerged in the 1860s after the Civil War, is the oldest and most persistent violent white-supremacist organization to tout this theory.

In Europe, extremists are putting their words into action in the increasingly hostile climate surrounding immigrants and refugees. Among the targets for attack are mosques, boardinghouses for immigrants, and reception centers for asylum seekers, while individual immigrants or refugees are harassed, threatened, beaten, and sometimes even murdered.

On a different level, biological racism, in the form of theories of superior and inferior human races, still occasionally comes up in some academic circles.

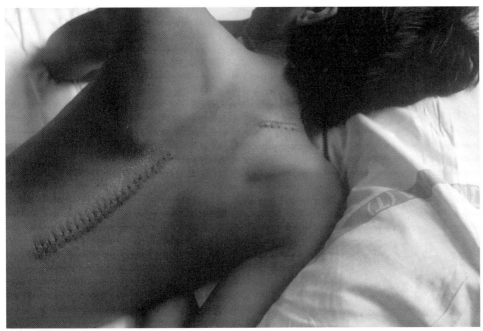

214 The slogan "Out with all foreigners" defiles a mosque in Huizen, the Netherlands, March 1992.
215 The scars of racial violence on the back of a fourteen-year-old Asian boy, London, July 1984.
216 Neo-Nazis attack Vietnamese people with axes, Berlin, 1990.

215

216

217

217 *Members of the Ku Klux Klan—an extreme right-wing white-supremacist organization.*

218 The funeral of the victims of an arson attack, Solingen, Germany, June 1993. Four skinheads were charged with the crime. Neighbors reported hearing the arsonists shout, "Heil Hitler."

219 Stephen Lawrence, eighteen, was stabbed to death at a bus stop in what was apparently a racially motivated attack, London, April 1993. Police were unable to prosecute Lawrence's killers and were accused of racism themselves for the mishandling of the case.

218

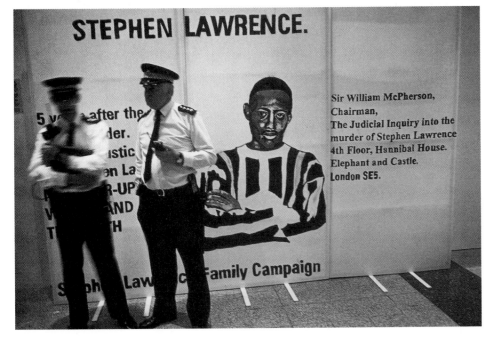

219

136

All over Europe, new nationalist parties are gaining support. They rally for what they call their "own people," the "true inhabitants," or those who "really belong" to a nation, state, town, or area. The consequence of their aim to put a certain group first is always the exclusion of various other groups from public life.

There is a thin line between patriotism, nationalism, and exclusion. Minorities are easy targets, especially when they are visibly different from the majority. The war in the former Yugoslavia has shown that the combination of extreme nationalism and civil war can quickly develop into mass murder and genocide, destroying social life and friendship even in cities where people of different backgrounds have lived together for generations.

221

220 *A demonstration held by the Vlaams Blok (Flemish Bloc), a right-wing extremist party in Belgium.*
221 *Jörg Haider, leader of Austria's far-right Freedom Party, holding an Austrian flag at the ski resort of Klagenfurt on his fiftieth birthday, January 2000.*
222 *Jean-Marie Le Pen, the leader of the French National Front, visiting the Movimento Sociale Italiano (Italian Social Movement).*

222

223

223 *The people of Srebrenica protest in shock and despair. Thousands of Muslim men and boys in this Bosnian village—falsely believed to be under the protection of UN troops— were deported and killed by Serbian troops in July 1995.*
224 *The Russian extreme nationalist politician Vladimir Zhirinovsky visiting Serbian troops in Bosnia, January 1994.*
225 *One of the victims of the nail bomb that exploded in a bar in Soho, London, in April 1999, waiting for medical help. Three people died in the attack, which targeted homosexuals.*

Who has not overheard comments such as "All Jews are . . ." or "All blacks are . . ." or "All gays are . . ."? From early childhood on, we all come across social stereotypes—in comics and schoolbooks, movies and newspapers. Prejudices develop when people hold on to negative stereotypes.

Prejudices are voiced in everyday conversations, but they can also be misused for political purposes. Widespread prejudice and a lack of opposition from many non-Jews made the Nazis' systematic persecution of Jewish people possible. The same was true for Gypsies and homosexuals. Anti-Semitic and other religious and racist prejudices are still present today in nearly every country in the world, and combating them is not solely the responsibility of national governments. It is also up to individuals. It is up to all of us.

226 A "No travelers" sign outside an English pub is meant to discourage Gypsies from entering, July 1999.
227 A demonstration against racism in London, October 1993.
228 "We are afraid": Austrian young people demonstrate against the inclusion of the Freedom Party in the new government, Vienna, February 2000.

228

PICTURE CREDITS

The publisher wishes to thank the following for permission to reproduce copyrighted material. All possible care has been taken to trace the ownership of material included and to make full acknowledgment for its use. If any errors have occurred, they will be corrected in subsequent printings.

ABC Press, Amsterdam *41, 44*

Algemeen Nederlands Persbureau, The Hague *212, 214, 218, 223, 227*

The Anne Frank Fonds/The Anne Frank House, Basel/Amsterdam *1, 2, 3, 4, 5, 6, 7, 8, 9, 10, 11, 12, 13, 104, 105, 106, 107, 108, 109, 110, 111, 112, 113, 114, 115, 116, 117, 118, 119, 120, 121, 165, 166, 167, 168, 169, 170, 172, 173, 206, 207, 208*

Luigi Baldelli/Transworld, Amsterdam *222*

G. Barclay/Corbis Sygma/ABC Press, Amsterdam *213*

Bildarchiv Abraham Pisarek, Berlin *86, 87, 88, 89*

Bildarchiv Preussischer Kulturbesitz, Berlin *57*

Charles Breijer/Nederlands Fotoarchief, Rotterdam *145, 155, 195*

Bundesarchiv, Koblenz *23, 59, 61, 62*

C. Carrion/Corbis Sygma/ABC Press, Amsterdam *211*

Violette Cornelius/Nederlands Fotoarchief, Rotterdam *160*

Gert Eggenberger/EPA/Algemeen Nederlands Persbureau, The Hague *221*

Jürgen Escher, Herford *184*

Gemeentearchief Amsterdam *127, 128, 129, 130, 137, 138, 179, 180*

Gemeentearchief Rotterdam *153, 199*

Historisches Museum Frankfurt, Frankfurt am Main *14, 15, 16, 18, 19, 21, 32, 34*

David Hoffman, London *215*

Institut für Stadtgeschichte, Frankfurt am Main *36, 71, 78, 203*